Moon Magic

Teresa Moorey

RIDER

LONDON · SYDNEY · AUCKLAND · JOHANNESBURG

First published in 2003 by Rider,
an imprint of Ebury Press, Random House,
20 Vauxhall Bridge Road, London SW1V 2SA

Random House Australia (Pty) Limited
20 Alfred Street, Milsons Point, Sydney,
New South Wales 2061, Australia

Random House New Zealand Limited
18 Poland Road, Glenfield,
Auckland 10, New Zealand

Random House South Africa (Pty) Limited
Endulini, 5A Jubilee Road,
Parktown 2193, South Africa

The Random House Group Limited Reg. No. 954009

Papers used by Rider are natural, recyclable products
made from wood grown in sustainable forests.

Printed and bound in Denmark by
Nørhaven Paperback A/S, Viborg

A CIP catalogue record for this book
is available from the British Library

ISBN 1-8441-3030-4

Welcome to the Little Book of Moon Magic!

The Moon is our guide in the realms of enchantment. Wise, gentle, fascinating and eerie, she is Queen of the fluctuating forces that govern our lives. Tuning into the Moon helps us to harmonise with our own instincts and natural rhythms. Rediscover what the ancients knew well – that the Moon rules magic …

Teresa Moorey

The Moon's Phases

Become well acquainted with the
Moon by watching her phases and noting
how you react to them, from New Moon
through to Full, Waning and back to New
again. It takes 29½ days for the Moon
to pass through this cycle.

When the New Moon appears in the
evening sky, you can cup the silver sickle in
your right palm in the Northern Hemisphere
or in your left in the Southern Hemisphere.

As the days progress the Moon rises later
and later, and when she is full she rides
high in the sky at midnight.

When the Moon is waning she can
be seen in the small hours, gradually
disappearing into the dawn.

The 'Dark of the Moon' is the time between
the disappearance of the waning Moon
and the reappearance of the New Moon,
when the Moon cannot be seen.

The Moon becomes 'new' in the middle
of her dark period. She is invisible at this
time because she is too close to the Sun.
We see the first sickle of New Moon as she
begins to draw away from the Sun
at the start of a fresh cycle.

The Moon always keeps the same
side turned towards us – we
never see her other face.

Befriending
The Moon

Keep a lunar diary to discover how the
Moon affects your feelings and actions. In it,
note down your dreams, how your energy
levels fluctuate, your state of health, how
much you accomplish, your relationships
with others and anything else that seems
important. Make a special note of any
intuitive insights or paranormal events.

You may also like to record the reactions
of your partner, friends, children, pets
and even plants!

Keep an eye on newspaper headlines –
do these reflect the Moon's phases?

After a few months you will come to
sense the powers of the Moon and how
these powers affect not only you, but the
subtle energy-field that surrounds us all.
Then you will be better placed to use
this energy in your lunar magic.

Strange Moons

BLUE MOON is a rare event when a Full Moon occurs twice in one month, with the first Full Moon being right at the beginning of the month. The term is also used for a Full Moon occurring twice in a row in the same sign of the Zodiac.

HARVEST MOON is the golden Full Moon that we see in September. At this time of year the Moon rises slowly, hanging close to the horizon for longer than usual. The atmosphere acts like a magnifying glass and makes the Moon look like a great amber balloon.

HUNTER'S MOON is similar, but refers to a Full Moon in October. Stags rut and there is increased animal activity in preparation for winter.

ECLIPSES occur when the Sun and Moon are in line with the earth. A lunar eclipse only happens at Full Moon when the Earth gets between the Sun and Moon, and the Moon appears to turn blood red at midnight. A solar eclipse only happens at New Moon when the Moon gets between the Sun and Earth. Because the Moon is relatively small, solar eclipses are rarely total. Eclipses were regarded as evil portents in ancient times. The Australian Aborigines believe that an eclipse of the Moon means that someone on a journey has come to harm.

The Moon's phase and eclipses are noted in newspapers. See how the next eclipse makes you feel.

The Moon
and The Tides

The Moon has always been associated
with water; in fact, the Aztec words for
'water' and 'Moon' were interchangeable,
and even land-locked peoples have often
associated her with the fall of dew.

Although the ancient Greeks did not
understand gravity, they knew the Moon
caused the tides. Many ancient peoples
believed that the affairs of humans
were also tidal.

High tide arrives with the passage
of the Moon overhead and another
comes 12 hours 25 minutes later, when
the Moon reaches the opposite point
beneath the Earth.

'Spring tides' occur at New and Full Moon.
Tides are higher when the Moon is closest
to the Earth and also at the Equinoxes.

While it is unlikely that the gravity
of the Moon could affect us directly,
there is little doubt that our bodies are
'tidal' in a more subtle sense, for life
responds to the Moon.

Werewolves and Vampires

A werewolf is a person who turns into a wolf when the Moon is full. Like many myths, this one has a basis in reality, for the Full Moon brings out the wild and instinctual in all of us. It is interesting that this 'lunar' creature can be killed only by a silver bullet – the Moon's metal.

Vampires cannot bear the light of the Sun, so must exist by that of the Moon. These mythical creatures embody deep symbolic and psychological meanings. One of the things the vampire represents

is all that is pushed into the darkness,
but which refuses to die.

Lunar wisdom teaches that we should
open our hearts and our imaginations, not
to judge but to understand. By being open
and accepting, we can enable the things
we fear to come out of the shadows,
transform and be reborn, as the
Moon is every month.

Living By The Moon

Living by the Moon may mean that your life runs more smoothly, and that you feel healthier and more energetic.

NEW MOON: make plans and new beginnings, or make a new start on an established projects. Put new resolutions into practice.

WAXING MOON: now projects can get into their stride. Be careful of overdoing things. Direct your enthusiasm well. Get in touch with friends, be active. If you need to be

on a 'build-up' diet, now is the best time
for your body to absorb nutrients.

FULL MOON: bring things to fruition
and abandon what isn't working. Parties,
outings, events, cooking in bulk,
love-fests – all go best now.

WANING MOON: analyse things, shed the
unnecessary, have a big sort-out. A detox
or reducing diet will work best now.

DARK MOON: enjoy a few quiet days;
think, reflect and start to plan
the next month.

Gardening By
The Moon

Plant life responds to the Moon's
phases – knowing about this will
give you green fingers.

FIRST SICKLE: plant seeds, especially herbs.

WAXING MOON: sow seeds over large
areas. Lay turf. Water with special care
because now the take-up of fluids is at its
best. Pick fruit and vegetables that you
are going to eat straight away.

APPROACHING FULL MOON: if the weather
has been dry, it's best to plant most seeds

now. Water once more. Pick fruit – it will
be succulent – also herbs and flowers.
Add fertiliser.

JUST AFTER FULL MOON: plant root veggies
like potatoes and carrots. Plant trees and
any flowers except annuals.

WANING MOON: attack those weeds!
Prune trees, mow the grass, start or increase
your compost heap. Pick plants that
need to be stored.

APPROCHING DARK MOON: spray
fruit-trees and cut timber.

Celebrate
The Moon!

Need an excuse for a party or outing? The
phases of the Moon can give you ideas.

NEW MOON is a great time for launching a
new project, meeting new friends, starting a
class or taking up a new sport or hobby.

FULL MOON is an exciting time for a big get-
together. Romances blossom and everyone
feels more hyped-up. Buy a big bunch of
flowers; pour yourself a glass of something
delicious and toast the Moon. Go to a gig
or concert and soak up the vibes.

WANING MOON is a wonderful sorting-out time. Get together with friends to weed gardens, strip wallpaper and have a quiet time chatting and relaxing into the evening with close companions.

DARK MOON is a quieter time. You may choose to spend it with your family or alone. Light a candle, burn some incense and reflect upon your life and your plans.

Moon-Children

Young children are fascinated by the
Moon and can learn about natural cycles
including the idea of death and rebirth
from watching her phases.

Celebrate the Full Moon with a party for
any children you know – or just for the
child in you! Have a cake with white icing
decorated with silver. Light a big, white
candle. Encourage your guests to talk about
the Moon, recite poetry, make up stories
and even to dress up and dance around
the garden in the moonlight.

If you are good at crafts, make a cardboard tiara with a circle bounded by two crescents pointing opposite ways, to represent the phases. Paint this with glue and sprinkle on silver glitter.

Take it in turns to be Moon Monarch, and say a party piece.

Kiss Your Hand
to The Moon

Kissing a hand to the Moon is an old
custom for bringing luck. You can also make
the ancient sign of the Horned God
(consort of the Moon) by bunching your
hand into a fist and then extending only
your index and little fingers, so your hand
looks like the head of a horned animal.
Hold this up towards the Moon so she
looks as if she is cradled between the
'horns'. This works best of all as a New
Moon greeting – a little act of worship that
you can follow by making a wish.

Drink To The Moon!

Lemons are ruled by the Moon. Make your own fresh lemonade from organic lemons, using 4 lemons, 5½ oz (120g) golden caster sugar and 2 pints (1140ml) of spring water. Squeeze the juice from the washed lemons and put the empty rinds in a large bowl. Boil the spring water, pour it over the rinds and add the sugar. Let it cool, strain, add the juice and chill. Raise your glass and drink down the lunar magic!

Making Moon Cakes

You can make these little cakes to celebrate the Full Moon. Eat them with a glass of white wine or grape juice, and some butter and jam.

You will need: 110g (4oz) butter – softened, 225g (8oz) golden granulated caster sugar, 2 free range eggs, 275g (10oz) organic plain flour, 1 tsp baking powder, 1 tsp salt, 1½ tbs organic honey, 1 tsp vanilla extract (natural), 1 tsp white wine or white grape juice, 2 tbs quick oats.

Mix the butter, sugar, eggs, honey, vanilla and wine thoroughly together. Blend in the flour, baking powder, oats and salt. Cover and chill for an hour, to make the dough easier to handle. Pre-heat the oven to 400° F, 200° C. Roll the dough out to the thickness of 5cm and cut into Full-Moon shapes with a pastry cutter. Bake for 6–8 minutes, until pale gold in colour.

Delicious!

Moon Meal Celebration

Hold a banquet for family and friends to celebrate Full Moon. Choose a spread of lunar foods such as milk, cheese, honey, white grape juice, white wine, cucumber, lettuce, white meat such as chicken, seafood (especially crustaceans), white bread and boiled potatoes. Follow this with a creamy, milky pudding. If you can, use silver dishes, napkins with an appropriate design and a white tablecloth. Put fragrant white flowers on the table – use your imagination and make your table as 'lunar' as possible. Light a white candle in the centre if possible in a bowl of water.

Use words of your own choosing,
such as 'Hail to the shining Goddess;
may her light fill our nights, our homes
and our hearts'. Each person can have their
own say. Women of child-bearing age
may wear silver crowns.

Improvise! Have fun!

De-Stress
With The Moon

Life in the fast lane can leave you strung out.
Create a lunar haven in your home where
you can relax and be your instinctual self.
All of these can create a lunar ambience:

A fish tank • silver objects • goddess
figures • pastels, blues, greens and violets •
plush upholstery and carpets • an indoor
fountain • prints and paintings of seascapes
and the Moon herself • crystal ornaments •
candles, soft lights • a tape or CD with
sounds of the ocean • jasmine in
an oil-burner

Retreat into your haven when the world has been harsh – but don't overdo it. You need to be able to bring your lunar inspirations back to the everyday world if you are to function.

A Lunar Scrapbook

Get in tune with the Moon by
making a lunar scrapbook.

Divide your book into four sections:
one for Dark Moon, one for Waxing Moon,
another for Full Moon and the fourth
for Waning Moon.

Collect pictures and mementoes to stick
in for the four phases. It doesn't matter
whether what you choose seems sensible
as long as it feels right to you. For instance,
you may wish to stick a picture of an old
woman in your Waning Moon section. Some
shiny silver coins might go in the Waxing

Moon pages. Or Dark Moon might show
lots of stars, for these are more visible
when the Moon has departed.

Pictures of goddesses and gods can also
go in your book, along with poetry,
meditations and spells.

Keep your book safe and secret.
Use it to get you in the right frame of
mind when you do your Moon magic.

An Altar
to Lady Moon

Create a shrine in your dwelling to the
Queen of the Night. If you need a logical
reason, tell yourself you are getting your
unconscious in tune with natural tides.
Otherwise, just enjoy!

Select a special shelf and cover it
with a silver or white cloth.

Decorate it with silver objects, for silver is
the Moon's metal. Animal figures are also
suitable and some 'lunar' animals include
dolphins, bears, dogs, cats and snakes.

Place candles there. You can choose
different colours for the different phases –
black for Dark Moon, white for Full Moon,
silver for New Moon, blue for Waning Moon.

Figures of goddesses such as Isis or
Diana could go on your altar, or the
Egyptian Moon-god, Thoth.

Burn a joss-stick to celebrate the Moon:
jasmine for Full Moon,
patchouli for Dark Moon.

Fresh flowers are lovely, or a simple goblet
of water honours the Moon's tidal power.

Don't be afraid to put anything on
your altar that 'feels right' to you.

Waning Moon Detox

Have you been overdoing it?
Feel that your body is full of toxins?
Poisons are more easily expelled as the
Moon wanes, so work with Doctor Moon
and give yourself a deep cleanse!

Just after Full Moon, cut out meat and dairy
produce; drink at least four pints (2 litres) of
water per day; eat organic fruits, vegetables
and cereals; cut out caffeine and alcohol;
exercise for twenty minutes a day and get
seven hours sleep per night.

When the next New Moon comes up you
too will feel like a new person! Guaranteed!

A Moon Rhyme

Modern Nature worshippers revive the old
ways and often link their celebrations to the
Moon, for she represents the Goddess and
shows us the cycle of rebirth in her
movements. Here is a chant suitable for
many festivals, including lunar ones:

We all come from the Goddess
And to Her we shall return;
Like a drop of rain
Flowing to the ocean.
Hoof and horn, hoof and horn –
All that dies shall be reborn.
Corn and grain, corn and grain –
All that falls shall rise again.
Isis Astarte Diana,
Hecate Demeter Kali
Inanna.

Maiden, Mother and Crone

The phases of the Moon depict the three
stages of womanhood. The Maiden is the
Waxing Moon, the Mother the Full Moon
and the Crone the Waning Moon.

Many goddesses are linked with
one specific lunar phase and one phase
of a woman's life. Equally there are many
triple goddesses such as the Three Graces,
or groups of three like that of the Greek
goddesses Persephone, Demeter
and Hecate.

At any age in a woman's life she can
make contact with any of the three stages,
contacting the wisdom of the Crone, the
generosity of the Mother or the freshness
of the Maiden – whichever she needs.

Simply use the brilliant Moon as a guide,
and light a candle – white for Maiden,
red for Mother, black for Crone.

Meditate, in the Moonlight if possible,
and feel yourself gently absorbing the
special qualities you require as the
Moonlight bathes the sky.

New Moon Ritual
to Persephone

Perspehone is the Maiden goddess
who was abducted by the Greek god
of the underworld, Pluto, to be his bride.
Her mother Demeter, the Earth goddess,
created winter in mourning. But the gods
decreed that Persephone should return
to her mother for half the year, and
so Spring returns with her.

When you see the first sickle of the
New Moon in the sky, light a white
candle and burn incense of lavender,
lemon peel and parsley. Have two
more white candles with you.

Hold up a shiny apple to the Moon or,
if you can, use a cut pomegranate instead,
for that was the fruit Persephone ate
in the Underworld. Say:

*'Lady Persephone, as you did eat of the
fruit of fertility so do I, embracing all
creative change that will come in this cycle.'*

Take a bite of the fruit. As you chew,
light the two other candles and say:

'This one is for what I must remember,'
and *'This one is for the future.'*

Re-light the candles each evening
until Full Moon. Bury what you
do not eat of the fruit.

Full Moon Ritual

You will need a large bowl, preferably made of silver, and a jasmine joss-stick or incense. If you cannot perform this ritual outside or indoors where the light of the Moon pours in, use either three candles or one large, thick, silver candle as a substitute for the moonlight.

Burn incense. Look at the reflection of the Moon in the water. Say:

'Lady of Dreams, be my inspiration;
Gypsy of the Skies, be my guide;
Queen of the Night, be my protector.'

Drink a little of the water. Immerse your hands in it, then anoint your face, eyes, lips, breast, belly, feet and any part of you that needs healing. If you wish to become pregnant trace a spiral of the water around your navel.

Pour any unused water onto the ground.

Dark Moon
Rite to Hecate

Hecate was a Titaness – a Greek goddess
even older than the Olympian pantheon.
She was goddess of magic and was
believed to stalk the highways and byways
when the Moon was dark. Crossroads
were especially sacred to her.

You will need a black candle; incense
or a joss-stick containing myrrh and/or
patchouli; a black stone such as onyx
or apache tear; a small silver bowl
containing water and a white candle.

Light the black candle and hold the stone in your hand. As you look deeply into it, think about the month gone by. Do you wish things had been different? What changes would you like to make? Maybe you are happy with the way it went and want things to continue in the same way. Ask Hecate to give you wisdom and self-knowledge.

When you are ready, wash the black stone in the water, light the white candle from the black and give thanks to Hecate for anything you have realised.

The Moon Rules

Those who work magic believe in a system of 'correspondences'. This means that if you use substances that 'correspond' to your purpose, your spell will work.

Lunar correspondences include:

COLOURS: white and silver

HERBS AND PLANTS: eucalyptus, lemon balm, calamus, camellia, camphor, coconut, lemon, gardenia, grape, jasmine, lily, lotus, mallow, Moonwort, myrrh, poppy, sandalwood, willow

STONES: pearl, beryl, aquamarine, crystal, moonstone, sapphire, selenite

METALS: silver

ANIMALS: dog, wolf, dolphin, bear, snake

These correspondences can be used in lunar spells for the home and healing, for children and fertility; for invoking the imagination, intuition, sleep, peace or prophetic dreams. Be creative – combine what you need for your purpose.

All is connected in the cosmic web.

Bach Flower Remedies

Bach flower remedies involve using delicate solutions of extracted plant material to help emotional problems. Try these Moon-ruled remedies:

WILLOW: to adjust to misfortune and adversity.

ASPEN: to calm vague and unknown fears you are afraid to talk about.

OLIVE: for treating exhaustion or the feeling that life is without pleasure.

VINE: for combating stress, feelings of hardness or callousness and the wish to coerce.

Witchy Thirteen

Why is thirteen 'unlucky for some'
but connected to witches and magic?

Because the Moon makes thirteen rounds of
the zodiac to one of the Sun, meaning there
are thirteen lunar months in the year.

If you are interested in hidden things
and magic, thirteen could be
your lucky number…

The Moon
and The Zodiac

Just as the Sun passes through all twelve
signs of the zodiac in one year, so the
Moon passes through them all in less than
a calendar month. It takes the Moon just
under 28 days to travel all the way round
the zodiac. Because the zodiac cycle of 28
days is less than the Moon-phase cycle of
$29\frac{1}{2}$ days, each month the Full Moon occurs
in the sign following the previous one.

The sign that the Moon was in when
you were born is almost as important as
your Sun sign, but to discover your Moon

sign you will need to consult special tables or get your birth chart drawn up.

Different sorts of magic may be best undertaken with the Full Moon in a specific sign of the zodiac – however, you don't have to wait if your need is urgent!

The Strength of The Moon

The Moon rules the Sun sign of Cancer.
People born under this sign are sensitive,
home-loving and caring.

Those born with the Moon in Cancer
in their horoscope may have very
powerful emotions.

The Moon is exalted in the sign of
Taurus. Those with the Moon in Taurus
have stable, warm feelings and are
very faithful and sensuous.

The Moon is in her detriment in Capricorn,
which is opposite Cancer. Those with the
Moon in Capricorn may be afraid of their
feelings, keeping them locked away.

The Moon is in her fall in Scorpio,
which is opposite Taurus. Those with the
Moon in Scorpio may have very intense
feelings that they find hard to express
in a positive manner.

Fire Moons

If you were born with the Moon in Aries,
Leo or Sagittarius, you have a fiery Moon.
You are enthusiastic about life and have
great faith in the future – although when you
get depressed everyone knows about it!
You have a sense of fun, love a bit of
drama, and you are passionate and
impulsive. To feel 'at home' you need a
sense of warmth, stimulation and
meaning in life.

Earth Moons

If you were born with the Moon in
Taurus, Virgo or Capricorn, you have an
earthy Moon. You are rooted in your body
and the evidence of your senses. You like
to be sure of your ground. It takes you a
while to respond but when you do, you
mean it! Sometimes you can be a little
over-cautious. To feel 'at home' you
need security, a sense of control and
knowledge of your resources.

Air Moons

If you were born with the Moon in Gemini,
Libra and Aquarius, you have an airy Moon.
You like to take life lightly and you are very
friendly and communicative. You may be
quick to respond but you are always just
that little bit detached – you aren't keen to
get emotionally involved. To feel 'at home'
you need to feel free, you need truth
and to know all is fair.

Water Moons

If you were born with the Moon in
Cancer, Scorpio or Pisces, you have a
watery Moon. Your feelings run very deep
and you do not always find it easy to
express them – you like to empathise and
to feel people understand and care. You
can be very emotional and just a touch
manipulative sometimes! To feel 'at home'
you need a feeling of belonging,
understanding and safety.

Zodiac Signs
and Magic

For working magic, the phase of the
Moon is generally more important than the
sign of the zodiac she occupies. And,
although it's easy to check lunar phases in
a newspaper, you will need an ephemeris
(a list of planetary tables) to know which
sign of the zodiac she is in. However, it's
easy to work out what sign of the zodiac
the Full Moon is in, because she is always in
the sign opposite to that occupied by the
Sun. All you need to know is the current
Sun sign, look at the zodiac wheel
and work from that.

If you want to give your magic some extra oomph, work it when the Full Moon is in a good sign for your purpose. But be adaptable! For instance, if you want more mental energy, why wait until the Full Moon appears in Gemini? Use the energies of Full Moon in one of the Fire Signs or in Virgo. You can alter your words to fit.

Moon in Aries Magic

A Full Moon that occurs between September 23rd and October 23rd will be in Aries. Use this time for any magic to do with:

sports, competition, taking first place • having exceptional energy • facing a challenge, overcoming obstacles • being brave • starting something completely new, particularly a new academic year • healing any ills of the head or treating headaches

Light a red candle and burn oil or
incense of cedarwood. Say:

*'Aries Moon, strong and bright,
Give to me the strength to fight.'*

Follow this with words of your own
choosing for your particular intent and finish
off by repeating the rhyme three times.

Moon in Taurus Magic

A Full Moon that occurs between October 24th and November 22nd will be in Taurus. Use this time for magic related to:

attracting wealth and material possessions • boosting creativity • enhancing sexuality and sexual attractiveness • the good things of life • security and stability or endurance • helping your garden through the winter months (if you live in the Northern Hemisphere) • healing connected with the neck and throat • boosting the immune system

Light a green candle and burn incense
or oil of patchouli or rose. Say:

'Taurus Moon, riding high,
All good things to me draw nigh.'

Follow this with words specific to your
intent and round off your ritual by
repeating the rhyme three times.

Moon in
Gemini Magic

A Full Moon that occurs between
November 23rd and December 21st will be
in Gemini. Use this time of sparkle, bright
ideas, jokes, laughter and repartee to:

bring light and life close to you as
Yuletide approaches • hold parties •
speed the post, make arrangements, swap
ideas • improve communication • chat
between friends, neighbours and siblings •
work with impartial and detached thinking
• travel short-distances • heal the
arms, hands and lungs

Light a pale yellow candle and burn
incense or oil of lavender. Say:

'Shining Moon in Gemini,
Light and life to me draw nigh.'

Follow this with more specific words
of your own and finish off by repeating
the rhyme three times.

Moon in Cancer Magic

A Full Moon that occurs between December 22nd and January 20th will be in Cancer. Use this time for helpful, quiet and domestic Moon for:

all matters to do with family, children, fertility • nurturing the imagination, dreams • working with the home, ancestors and tradition • matters of the sea or safety • holidays and family times in the Southern Hemisphere • healing the stomach and breasts, also the lymphatic system

Light a white candle and burn incense
or oil of eucalyptus or jasmine. Say:

'Moon in Cancer, pure and white,
Bring me times of true delight.'

Follow this with more specific words
connected to your intent and round off
by repeating the rhyme three times.

Moon in Leo Magic

A Full Moon that occurs between
January 21st and February 18th will
be in Leo. Use this time for:

matters concerning power, leadership,
success • creativity, determination • affairs
of the stage and entertainment • romantic
relationships and issues to do with children
• boosting or adding zest to late summer
plans in the Southern Hemisphere •
healing the heart and the chest

Light a gold or orange candle and
burn oil or incense of frankincense,
cinnamon or orange. Say:

'Leo Moon, I bow to you:
Give me success in all I do.'

Follow this with specific words about
your intent and finish off by repeating
the rhyme three times.

Moon in Virgo Magic

A Full Moon that occurs between February 19th and March 20th will be in Virgo. Use this Moon for:

getting organised • having a sort-out, tidying, cleaning • separating the wheat from the chaff • reviewing what you have achieved • catching up with small jobs and matters to do with your daily routine • cleansing and detoxing of all descriptions • healing the digestive system

Light a green or yellow candle and burn oil
or incense of lavender or mimosa. Say:

'Virgo Moon, crystal clear,
All things in their place appear.'

Follow this with specific words about your
purpose and complete with three-times
repetition of the rhyme.

Moon in Libra Magic

A Full Moon that occurs between March 21st and April 20th will be in Libra. This Moon is good for:

promoting justice and fairness • aiding arbitration and conciliation • resolving breaches and enabling relationships to go smoothly • partnership or legal matters and also for bonds of love • helping people air their differences and find agreement • creating tact, diplomacy and balance • healing of the kidneys.

Light a blue candle and burn incense
or oil of rose or geranium. Say:

*'Moon in Libra, fair to see,
Bring balance, peace and love to me.'*

Complete this with words of your own
choosing specific to your cause and finish
off by repeating the rhyme three times.

Moon in Scorpio Magic

A Full Moon that occurs between
April 21st and May 21st will be in Scorpio.
Use this Moon for:

intense emotional matters such as
purging guilt, lust or obsession • keeping
things secret • solving mysteries and getting
to the root of things • concentration and
exam revision • seeing deep within •
dealing with sexual matters • healing
the sexual organs

Light a deep-red candle and burn incense
or oil of myrrh or ginger. Say:

'Scorpio Moon, rising from the Deep,
Help me all my power to keep.'

Finish this off with words appropriate to
your special purpose and complete it by
repeating the rhyme three times.

Moon in Sagittarius Magic

A Full Moon that occurs between May 22nd and June 21st will be in Sagittarius. This Moon is helpful for:

the acquisition of wisdom and understanding • adventures, both mental and physical • travel that truly broadens the mind • expanding the conceptual horizons and getting the 'big picture' • long-term planning • 'rising above' spirituality • long-distance journeys • healing arthritis and other ills in the hips and thighs

Light a purple candle and burn incense
or oil of clove or sandalwood. Say:

'Archer Moon in Heaven's height,
Help my soul now to take flight.'

Finish this off with specific words for
your purpose and repeat the rhyme
three times to complete the spell.

Moon in Capricorn Magic

A Full Moon that occurs between June 22nd and July 22nd will be in Capricorn. This Moon is useful for:

career matters • anything to do with status or the establishment of a reputation • map-reading, planning and organising • binding and grounding • containing or ending • doing what is necessary without becoming emotionally incapable • healing of the knees

Light a dark blue candle and burn incense
or oil of cypress or patchouli. Say:

*'Capricorn Moon, bright and round,
Keep my feet upon the ground.'*

Follow this with special words for
your purpose and finish off by repeating
the rhyme three times.

Moon in Aquarius Magic

A Full Moon that occurs between July 23rd and August 23rd will be in Aquarius. This Moon is for wishes to come true and it can help with:

creating detachment • inspiration and keeping a broad, unbiased outlook • humanitarian and charitable matters • telepathy and mental ingenuity • expanding a social circle and getting together with friends • healing problems with the ankles

Light a bright blue candle and burn
incense or oil of lavender or pine. Say:

'High Moon in Aquarius,
Grant me something marvellous!'

Now follow this with specific words of
your choosing and finish the spell by
repeating the rhyme three times.

Moon in
Pisces Magic

A Full Moon that occurs between
August 24th and September 22nd will be
in Pisces. This psychic Moon helps with:

the expansion of consciousness • mysticism
and understanding dreams – or dreaming
true • divination and clairvoyance •
escapism and 'getting away from it all' •
feeling laid back and relaxed • boosting the
imagination • healing of the feet or matters
involving bodily fluid balance.

Light a violet or turquoise candle and
burn incense or oil of ylang-ylang,
eucalyptus or sage. Say:

'Moon in Pisces, bright your beam,
Bring to me my sweetest dream.'

Finish this off with words appropriate to
your specific purpose and complete the
spell by repeating the rhyme three times.

Looking Into
The Future

If you want to become a seer,
the Moon can lead you!

Take a large, deep bowl of water and sit
with it between your legs, with the
reflection of the Moon falling in it.

Burn a jasmine joss-stick, but all around
you should be in darkness.

Take a deep breath, close your eyes and
frame your question, clearly and simply.

Open your eyes and stare at the Moon
in the water. Look deep, deep within,
at the shining, mysterious Moon.

The water may cloud over and you
may see figures form. Or you may go
into a dreamy state and the pictures
form inside your head.

Be sure to take note of everything you see,
but do not try to work it out – just watch.

Later on you will be able to interpret,
and find your answer!

Lunar Libromancy

Need a quick answer to a question?
There is a very simple way to divine.
All you need is a book and the influence
of the Moon's phase.

Choose a general book that covers
plenty of life-areas – poetry is good,
or a child's encyclopaedia.

If your question is about outer matters
such as 'Does he/she love me?' or 'Which
career path should I take?', choose the
time of Full Moon to ask the oracle. If your
question is an inward one about knowing
yourself and your feelings, such as

'Am I really happy here?' or 'Can I really trust...?', choose Dark Moon.

Close your eyes, hold the book on your lap and let the pages run past your fingers, until you feel like stopping.

Open your eyes and the first phrase you see on the page will hold your answer.

Boost Your Intuition

Intuition is a natural thing! Candles
and incantations are fine, but we develop
true contact with our instincts by spending
time in the places where they are
really at home – in nature.

If you want to deepen your understanding
and develop as a seer, take regular walks
when the Moon is in the sky. Look at her,
watch her in all her moods and phases. See
how the world looks when bathed in the
silver glow of Full Moon. Touch trees to see
how they 'feel' at Full Moon. Watch the way
animals and birds behave and be aware of
the resonance of the earth beneath your feet.

Let your inner eye open in
response to the Moon!

A Lunar Bouquet

Gather an armful of fragrant Moon flowers to
celebrate Full Moon. Include lilies, camellia,
gardenia, jasmine, poppies and some sprigs
of willow if you can. All or any will do –
include other white flowers if you like.
(Although roses are strictly ruled by Venus,
white roses may have lunar links.)

Smell the fragrance and draw the
subtle beauty of the Moon within you.
Arrange the flowers on your altar, or
place in a shaded corner of your room,
to invite the Moon inside.

Moon Runes

In ancient times an alphabet was much more than a collection of sounds. People understood that all is vibration and that in the cosmic spectrum everything is linked. So alphabets had magical meanings.

The Runic alphabet was used by the Vikings, and its symbols were revered. Two runes in this alphabet had strong connections with the Moon:

ALGIZ [ᛉ] links with the yew tree, and with the qualities of protection, meditation and healing. Meditating upon it can give you insight. Focussing on it can help your

career, creativity and friendship, and put
you in charge of your emotions.

OTHILA [ᛟ] links with the hawthorn and
with your home and property. Meditating
upon it can help you feel that you belong,
and help you put down roots. Focussing on
it is good for marriage and children, and for
connecting with your spiritual heritage

Moon Numbers

Ancient people – and modern
numerologists! – believe that numbers
do not just convey quantity. They also have
a 'quality', a vibrational signature, forming
part of the cosmic web that surrounds us.

The number 2 is lunar, for the Moon
is the second brightest light in the sky after
the Sun, and in her phases the Moon has
two horns. The ancients believed that 2 was
a very feminine, receptive number,
sometimes subtle and scheming but
very sweet and even-tempered.

Each of us has several important personal numbers. You can discover yours by: adding together the digits of your birthday (e.g. for the 29th = 2+9 = 11 = 1+1 = 2) adding up the digits of your entire birth date (i.e. the numbers of the month, day and year) the numerical correspondences of your name (each letter can be converted to a number, starting with A =1 etc. up to I = 9, and then starting with J =1 again).

Do you have many 2s in your numerical make-up? Then you are a gentle Lunarian. Any 2s in your address or phone number will bring co-operation and domestic balance.

Lunar Alchemy

Alchemy was popular in the Middle Ages
and lots of mysterious diagrams and
writings on the subject survive, many of
which include lunar symbols. Alchemy was
more than an attempt to turn base metals
into gold – it was a spiritual quest.

The alchemist's power came from
the *conjunctio* – the union of the King
and the Queen. The King was symbolised
by the Sun, the Queen by the Moon. This is
a reminder to look deep within ourselves,
to the balance of male and female, yin and
yang, inside. Without balance there can

be no creativity; without true awareness of
ourselves there can be no progress.

Let the Moon teach you to look within,
as she has taught so many through
the centuries.

The Moon in The Tarot

The Tarot can be used for divination
and for self-development. In the Tarot,
the Moon is card number 15 of the
Major Arcana and it is associated
with the astrological sign of Pisces.

The card may appear in any of a multitude
of designs, depending on the deck, but it
will always show the Moon and may
display other associated images such as the
sea, baying dogs or other lunar creatures.

In a spread, the Moon card can mean illusion, confusion and self-deception. However, reflecting upon this card can help you to develop psychism and to increase your awareness of dream meanings and your connection with natural rhythms. It triggers an ability to 'go with the flow' and to be aware of our roots in the time before time, when instincts were strong.

To make contact with your inner wisdom, and to avoid the self-deception that this card can imply, prop the Moon card where you can see it while you meditate. Light a purple candle and let your awareness deepen.

The Moon in Your Hand

The mounts on the hand denote
certain characteristics and are
named after the planets.

The Mount of Luna, or the Moon,
is found towards the outside of the palm,
just above the wrist, opposite the thumb.

If the mount is high and well-formed, the
intuition, imagination and psychic faculties
are likely to be pronounced.

These characteristics will be even more prominent if a star formation or other special marking appears on this mount.

The Line of Intuition – when present – encircles the mount and signifies marked psychic and mediumistic ability.

Where the Head Line (the lower of the two main lines that cross the palm) bends down toward the Mount of Luna, logic gives way before the emotions – guard against depression and illusion, and follow your heart.

Moon Angel

The angel of the Moon is Gabriel, whose
name means 'Strength of God'.

This archangel is a messenger, awakening us
to cosmic truth, and appears many times in
the Bible as a harbinger of creative change.
Gabriel also parted the waters of the Red
Sea so that the Hebrews could escape from
Egypt, suggesting a connection with the
tides and with passage. Islamic tradition
states that Gabriel, being the Angel of Truth,
revealed the Koran to Mohammed.

Often depicted holding a lily – which is ruled by the Moon – or a sceptre, this angel may be male or female. S/he brings the gifts of psychism, seeing and hearing, fertility and balance. Gabriel comes to us in dreams, whispering those special things we need to know.

Invoke Gabriel with incense or oils of jasmine and/or mimosa, and by wearing a fire opal.

Willow Lore

The willow is ruled by the Moon, and
willow roots will often extend far
underground in search of water.

This lunar tree is sacred to the Chinese
goddess of compassion, Kuan Yin, who
uses a willow branch to sprinkle
the waters of life.

The willow also signifies death,
which is part of the cycle of re-growth.

The tree is also associated with rejection
in love. The custom of wearing the green
willow around a hat when love is lost may

originate from a charm against the jealousy of the Moon goddess. The Moon is about emotions, which may be changeable and fickle, and also about the ways in which we may deceive ourselves. But on the other hand, if you want to attract love, carry a willow-leaf!

Willow bark and sandalwood may be burnt together as incense under a waning Moon to call up spirits.

A New Broom

The plant broom (*cytisus scoparius*)
is said by some to be ruled by the Moon.
Witches use a besom made from this plant
for sweeping out their circle in ritual
cleansing, before magic.

It was the plant behind the heraldic design
of the Plantagenet family, who were said
to be involved in the magical arts.

If you are plagued by poltergeists and
restless spirits, make an infusion of broom
by steeping the plant substances in hot
water – the proportions are not crucial.
Sprinkle this around your property, saying,

'Plant of broom so strong,
Rid me of all that's wrong,
Keep me and mine safe and sound,
By your magic all around.'

Incense

You do not have to use incense
but it often helps to create the right
atmosphere for spells if you do.

For your Moon rites, choose a silver
censer or heat-proof dish for your incense
(*do not* use an old ashtray as this
will not be strong enough).

Obtain charcoal discs from a New Age
shop. Hold one in tongs, against a flame,
until it sparks and begins to go grey. Lay the
disc flat in your censer and sprinkle your
incense in the centre.

A New Moon blend can contain
lavender, lemon balm and calamus.

A Full Moon blend can contain
frankincense, sandalwood and
rose (petals or essence).

A Waning/Dark Moon blend can contain
Myrrh, cypress, copal and/or Orris root.

The Olive Tree

The olive is sacred to the Moon, and
Gabriel, the angel of the Moon, is often
shown with an olive branch.

Greek brides wore a crown of olives for
fertility and olive leaves can be scattered to
bring peace and tranquillity.

The olive leaf symbolises the renewal of life.
Carry an olive leaf for luck, and share olives
with your lover, for they are an aphrodisiac!

Magic Monday

Monday is the 'Moon's Day' – that is the origin of the name. This is also true in French, *Lundi* being the day of *la lune*.

Monday is the traditional day for spells for love and togetherness, for healing hurts, family matters, gardening, travel, anything to do with water or the sea, and for 'the sight'.

The third hour after sunset is the best time for rituals.

If the Full Moon falls on, or just after Monday, this is an especially powerful occasion magically.

Magic Circle

All magic is best performed inside
a ritual circle, which gives protection
and concentration.

For your Moon magic, make your circle
by directing energy with your forefinger,
clockwise, in a circle around you.
Visualise it as blue light.

Your circle should be guarded by the four
Elemental Powers at the four quarters. These
powers are associated with lunar phases:

NORTH is Earth and Dark Moon.
Light a black candle.

EAST is Air and Waxing Moon.
Light a silver candle.
SOUTH is Fire and Full Moon.
Light a red or white candle.
WEST is Water and Waning Moon.
Light a blue candle.

Now you have the symbolic presence of all
the phases and elements to strengthen any
rite. Always mentally dismantle your circle
when you have finished, and give thanks.

(N.B In the Southern hemisphere,
swap the North/South elements and
phases and move anti-clockwise
when creating your circle.)

Lunar Togetherness

Have you and your other half been
going through a hard time lately?
Let the Moon bring you close again.

When the Moon is full, fill a large
bowl with fresh water. Add some
drops of rose or jasmine oil, or
float white rose-petals on top.

Let the Full Moon reflect in the water as you
both sit near the bowl. Put your hands in it,
play with the water and with each other's
fingers. Hold hands, caress, say nothing …

Now begin gently to trace the Moon-water over the face of your lover – forehead, eyes, lips. Linger as long as you like, then progress to other parts of the body.

No need for words –
let your fingers do the talking!

Traveller's Moon

The Moon is a wanderer,
but she always returns.

If you have to go far away from home
for any length of time, try this spell to keep
you safe and attached to your roots.

You will need a length of cord,
seven silver beads, seven white beads
and a large silver candle.

Starting at New Moon, light your candle in
the evening and thread one white bead on
your cord, naming something good about
your home that you want to retain. The next

night thread a silver bead, naming it for
something you hope to gain from your
travel. Continue alternately with each
evening that follows.

At Full Moon thread your last
silver bead and knot the cord round
your candle. Let it burn down.

Keep your cord-charm with you as you
roam – you will never be far from home.

Lunar Healing

Healing magic is a lunar province.

To send someone well-being, ask their permission to help. Choose a Waxing Moon to work this charm. Anoint a green candle with eucalyptus oil or ring it with a eucalyptus wreath. Imagine the person smiling and joyful. Say:

'As the shining Moon does swell,
So may [name] be happy and well.'

You may do this each evening until Full Moon. Then, why not raise a glass of wine or grape juice to the Moon in thanks – along with your fully-recovered friend!

Lunar Luck

Know when the New Moon is due to arrive?
It is especially lucky to see it for the first
time over your right shoulder.

Look out for the first New Moon in the
New Year. When you see it, speak your
wish out loud – it will be fulfilled.

The first Full Moon is lucky too – it will make
your wish materialise before the year ends.

To See Your
True Love

Wait for the first Full Moon of the New Year.
Go out to where the reflection of the Moon
falls on a pool or stretch of water.

Look for your reflection there. Allow
yourself to feel relaxed and dreamy. The
face of your future love will be reflected
back at you, beside your own.

Wishing Moon

Write your wish on a bay-leaf when the
Moon is new. (The writing doesn't have to
be clear or detailed – initials will do, as
long as *you* are very clear about your wish.)

Hold the leaf to your forehead
while you look at the Moon,
imagining your wish materialising.

Sleep with the bay leaf under your pillow.

To Deter Troublesome Neighbours

Take a small hand-mirror and leave it out in the light of the Full Moon for several nights until the Moon has started to wane. (N.B: It does not matter if the Moon is behind cloud for much of the time, as long as it has been caught in Moonlight at least once.)

Hold the mirror in your right hand and say:

*'Trouble come is trouble turned –
Peace and love to all concerned.'*

Place the mirror on a windowsill, facing towards your nasty neighbours.
Relax! Your shield is in place!

To Find A
New Home

When you see the first silver crescent in
the sky, light a white candle that you have
anointed with a little lavender oil. Visualise all
the things you want in your new home. Say:

'Moon, as you sail o'er Heaven's dome,
Spy for me a lovely home
Where I can be happy, where I can rest.
O Wandering Moon, now do your best!'

Light the candle every night
until the Moon is full. Repeat
next month, if necessary.

To Break A Curse

In fact, the vast majority of 'curses'
exist only in the mind of the one 'cursed'
by reason of their own negativity.
Nonetheless, this will help …

Choose the first Saturday of the waning
Moon and light a black candle. Say:

*'I return all that is dark and evil to this black
candle. As it burns down so will all that is
harmful to me burn away and be destroyed.
Ashes to ashes, dust to dust, so mote it be.'*

Burn each night until the candle is gone
and/or the Moon has disappeared from the
sky. Bury any leftover wax in the garden.

Money Moon

There are many lunar spells
you can do to attract wealth.

When the Moon is new, place a bank-note of
the largest sum you afford underneath the
doormat at your front door. Remove it only
when the Moon is full and return it there at
the next New Moon if you like. The larger the
bank-note the greater the dividend – and the
more feet that walk over it the better!

Alternatively, place as much money
as you can on your windowsill in
the light of the New Moon. Say:

'O magic Moon, make my money grow.'

You can repeat this also
at the next New Moon.

Folk Spell
For Money

When you see the very first silver
sickle – not through glass – turn over the
silver coins in your pocket and say:

*'In the name of the Great Mother,
the Horned God and the Magical Child,
may my money grow this month!'*

Now fortune is on its way!

Moonwort
Money Spells

This herb is ruled by the Moon.
Place a sprig of moonwort in your
purse to attract more silver.

Place it in a box at the back of your
cupboard and wealth will come to you.

Burn dried moonwort at the New Moon.
Watch the vapours rise and imagine the
wealth that will soon be yours.

Sandalwood Spells

Fragrant sandalwood is ruled by the
Moon. It is used as incense especially for
spells for healing, protection and exorcism.
Mix with frankincense for a Full Moon rite.

Take a large chip of sandalwood
and write a wish on it. Burn this in a
heat-proof dish, visualising your wish
as you do so, to make it come true.

Wear beads made of sandalwood for
protection and spiritual development.
Leave them in the light of the Full Moon
occasionally, for extra power.

Willow Wedding?

Moon-ruled willow can give you an
answer about your love-life. To find out if
you will have a relationship over the coming
year, throw your shoe into a willow tree.
You can have nine tries in all, and if your
shoe catches you will be with your
love by the end of the next year.

Give this a try at a party next New Year's Eve
– but remember, you're going to have to
climb that tree to get your shoe back!

Watchful Wintergreen

Wintergreen is a Moon herb,
and will protect children if a little
is placed inside their pillow case.
It can bring them life-long good fortune.

Mix it with mint and sprinkle around
the house to remove bad vibes.

Coconut Nice!

Coconut is ruled by the Moon. Your home
will remain safe if you hang a coconut in it.
But if you don't fancy this hairy ornament,
then cut a coconut in two, drain it and fill
the inside with a selection of protective
herbs such as clove, frankincense, rosemary,
mint and eucalyptus. Seal it back up
and bury it in the garden.

Workplace Magic

Fed up with the rat-race? Would you prefer to be at home, where it's safe and peaceful? The Moon understands.

Find yourself a clear crystal. Place it out, or on your windowsill, in the light of the Full Moon. Ask the Moon for calmness and serenity, and for protection from back-biting and office politics.

Next morning take your crystal to work
and put it on your desk. Take a minute
to recall the peace of the Full Moon.
Imagine your charged-up crystal is
projecting a force-field around you, like
a crystal egg, shielding you from negativity.
Then get on with your work in peace.

Recharge your crystal at each Full Moon.

Waning Moon
Spell for Justice

Is someone treating you unfairly or
trying to make you go against your beliefs?
Do this spell at the Waning Moon.

Make a circle of sage leaves,
dried or fresh. In the middle place
something that symbolises the subject
matter, such as a coin for money, ring for
partnership, model house for property, etc.

Sprinkle some sage onto your symbol and
follow with a sprinkle of lavender drops for
wisdom and clear communication. Bind the

symbol round and round with black thread, seeing your resentment and all the troubles being 'bound up' along with it.

Leave this on your window-ledge until the first crescent of the Moon appears. Take it outside and unbind it, seeing all the negative issues take flight. Bury the cord in the ground along with your symbol – or if this is to be used again, wash it in a running stream. Go forward with a clear head and light heart.

Salt Spell for Protection

The Moon-ruled sea is salty,
and salt has many ritual uses involving
cleansing and protecting.

Fill a clear vessel with spring water
and leave it out in full sunlight and the
light of the waxing Moon for a
twenty-four hour period.

Now dissolve some salt in the water.

Sprinkle this in the four corners of the room that needs to be protected. Sprinkle it also around the window and door.

If you need to protect an entire apartment, house and garden, sprinkle the mixture round the boundaries.

Lunar Love Spell

When the New Moon appears
in the sky find a heart-shaped petal,
preferably of a rose.

You will need some red or rose-pink paper
and a silver pen. Write on the paper:

*'As the fair Moon waxes to full,
My true love to me I pull.'*

Have a bath or shower and put on
a clean robe – or stand naked.

Light a rose-red candle and chant
your words three times, while you hold
the petal in the candle-glow.

Fold the paper round the petal and seal it
with some of the wax from the candle.
Place the paper somewhere safe.

By the time New Moon arrives again,
love should have come too.

Beauty and The Bath

Need a special boost
for an important date?

Choose the time when the Moon is just
approaching full. Light six candles in silver
holders around your bath. Three candles
should be rose pink, three white.
The bathroom should be warm.

Drop some rose oil and/or sprinkle rose
petals onto the surface of the bath water.
Burn a rose-scented joss-stick, or place
more of the oil in an oil burner.

Soft, sensuous music will help you relax. Close your eyes and imagine that your body is absorbing radiant beauty from the surrounding water. Just feel yourself glow! Imagine as many seductive situations as possible, where the lover of your dreams is totally smitten by you.

When you are ready to get out, wrap yourself a huge, soft, rose-coloured towel and get ready in a leisurely way, knowing that delights are to come!

Anger Begone!

Choose a Waning Moon for this spell
and, if you can, stay up until you can
see the Waning Moon in the sky.

Burn a black candle. Write down
all the things that are making you angry
on a piece of white paper with a black
pen. Get it all out! Then twist the paper into
a taper. Think of how good it will be
to be free of these thoughts.

Light the paper in the candle flame
and place it in a strong dish –
preferably black – to burn.

Carefully take the ashes out and cast
them at the Waning Moon, saying:

'Old Moon, on the wane
Take away my ire and pain.'

Sprinkle a little lavender oil on your
pillow and imagine all the good things
to come as you fall asleep.

White Wash

Are you dashing around too much, not giving yourself time to think, feeling cut-off, confused and stressed?

When the Moon is full and fair, take a white satin scarf out into the moonlight. Hold it resting on your arms. Face the Moon and close your eyes.

Feel the light of the Moon wash through you, cleansing away all the stress, muddles and anxiety. Let your mind go blank, breathe deeply and take the lunar glow deep inside you, opening your mind, making you calm and receptive.

Drape the scarf about you, come back inside, have a milky drink and wind down – do nothing for the rest of the evening.

Wear the white scarf whenever you need to chill. Recharge it with the same ritual next Full Moon, if you need to.

Faeries by Moonlight

The Irish know faeries as 'the People of the *Sidhe*' – beautiful and terrible creatures from another dimension. It is a great privilege to see faeries: do not be afraid but be very respectful.

One of the favourite traditional times to see faeries is by the light of the Full Moon. When the Full Moon shines on the trees of the Faery Triad – the oak and ash and thorn – then you may be especially likely to glimpse the Fair Folk.

A garden full of fragrant roses is sure to appeal to faeries – look for them at midnight by the light of the Moon.

But if you fear to see the Little People when you have to go abroad when the Full Moon is gleaming, then carry a sprig of gorse for protection.

Moon Stone ~ Beryl

Crystal balls used to be made
of this Moon-ruled stone.

Beryl can be worn to keep you safe when
travelling by sea. It guards against drowning
and also against sea-sickness.

Wearing beryl can help you resist
manipulation and coercion by salesmen
and evangelists.

Five hundred years ago, it was believed that
beryl could help the wearer to win debates
and still be liked and respected by all!

Beryl is exchanged by lovers so that their
love may remain true.

Moon Stone ~ Chalcedony

This milky white stone is ruled by the Moon.

It brings peace, calms fears and cheers
the heart, when held or worn.

It wards off black magic and all negativity.

It is especially useful for nursing mothers,
who can wear beads of chalcedony to
help stimulate the flow of milk.

Moon Stone ~ Crystal

There are many types of crystal, and it is, of course, the favourite substance for the 'crystal ball' although balls for divination can also be made of glass or of other stones such as amethyst. White, clear crystal is especially powerful for Moon magic, especially when set within silver.

To make your own miniature circle of power, choose a variety of white crystals and embed them in white or silver sand in a large dish. Or, if you are quite sure of your final design, you could set them in self-hardening modelling clay.

For your design, you could set the crystals in the pattern of astrological symbols such as a crescent for the Moon or the 'female' sign of a circle with a cross beneath for Venus. Or just do whatever feels right for you.

Use your crystal temple to 'charge' objects that you are going to use magically, such as charms and amulets. For instance, a piece of rose quartz set within the Venus sign and left out in the Full Moon would make a wonderful love charm.

Moon Stone ~ Geodes

All crystals take shape within geodes, which are hollow, often egg-shaped structures that may be very beautiful. They may be quite expensive, but make wonderful ornaments and magical objects.

Keep a geode in your bedroom while making love if you want to have a baby, but take it out before sleeping, as crystals can be powerful things.

Use a special geode as a focus
for meditation, catching the flickering
candle-glow – amethyst is especially
good for this – or place one on your altar
to amplify your energies when doing magic.
A geode on a lunar altar is a perfect
way to honour Lady Moon.

Moon Stone ~ Marble

Marble is made of lime and shares some similarities with coral. Marble is a protective substance. Place some marble on your altar if you are doing spells to shield you from attack of any sort, or carry a piece that you have 'charged up' by either leaving it in the light of the Full Moon or in a magical rite.

Marble is good for kitchen fittings as it brings the right lunar 'vibe' for cookery, domestic arts and security. Work surfaces with a marble finish aren't quite the same, so add a real marble chopping board for greater effect.

Moon Stone ~ Aquamarine

This blue-green stone has links with the sea.

Leave an aquamarine in a clear glass of fresh spring water, in the light of the Full Moon for several hours. Take out the stone with clean fingers and sip the water to cleanse you inwardly and to prepare you for magic or divination.

Moon Stone ~ Moonstone

Obviously with strong lunar associations, moonstone's powers are so linked to its namesake that these gems are said to wax and wane with the Moon in the heavens.

Moonstone is sacred to the Moon goddess and many witches like to wear it. It can be placed beneath your pillow for a restful sleep and sweet dreams, or a moonstone necklace can be worn in bed.

It is also protective and can be given to your friends when they go off on a trip, especially if travelling by sea.

Hold the stone in your hand as the Moon is waxing to full. Visualise the lunar power as a white light that beams down, surrounding the little stone and causing it to pulsate with protective energy. So great is the survival power of this little stone that the bearer cannot possibly come to harm!

Give it with love – and ask for a postcard in return!

Moon Stone ~
Mother-of-Pearl

This isn't really a 'stone' but the interior of the shells of sea molluscs. Avoid commercial mother-of-pearl because the creatures will have been killed to obtain it. Collect your own, if possible, in rock-pools and streams.

Empower a special piece of mother-of-pearl to give as a protective gift for a newborn baby – or you could simply use a clean sea-shell.

When the first silver sickle appears
in the sky, face the Moon and hold up
your piece of mother-of-pearl, and
visualise the sparkling light entering it.
Feel it tingling with power. Say:

*'New Moon, as you grow and shine, so may
this little one grow and thrive. Blessed Be.'*

Give it, wrapped in white satin,
to the parents.

Moon Metal ~ Silver

Silver has long been sacred to the Moon.
Witches and priestesses often wore silver
crescents in honour of the lunar Goddess.

Silver reflects negativity away from the
person who wears it, just as the Moon
reflects the light of the Sun. The 'horns'
of a silver crescent repel evil.

Silver is related to love, healing the
emotions and psychic abilities. Wearing
silver may attract love, but can cause you to
feel emotionally overwhelmed at the time
of the Full Moon – when wearing
gold can balance its effect.

Silver set with a stone ruled by the
Moon is a powerful lunar charm.
Those touched by silver are able to
shed anger and nervousness. A silver
ring can keep you calm.

Silver jewellery helps you sleep,
especially if set with Moonstone. It can
give you psychic dreams. Silver may also
be placed beneath the pillow for the same
effect. This metal also guards travellers,
especially those at sea.

To Get Rid
of A Problem

When the Moon is waning,
write your problem on a piece
of paper and burn it. Simple!

To End A Run
of Bad Luck

Check the Moon phases in a
calendar or diary and time this spell so
the last day you do it falls on the last day
of the waning Moon. Each day go for a walk
and pick up a piece of dried wood. Do this
for seven days. When the Moon is at her
darkest, bind the twigs with black
thread and burn them. Say:

*'Ill luck, your time has come to die;
A bright new phase is drawing nigh.'*

Lunar Law of Magic

Moon will wane and Moon will grow:
'Harm none' is the one rule you must know!

To see the Moon wax and wane,
flick through this book from back to front
if you live in the Northern Hemisphere, and
from front to back if you live in the Southern.